SHARDA GEER

101 Insights about the ego mind

An essential handbook for personal growth and development, enhancing self awareness

This book was professionally typeset on Reedsy.
Find out more at reedsy.com

I would like to dedicate this book to my family, for your unwavering support and love,
To my editor, Natalia for your keen eye and invaluable insights
and to my coach Master Coach Hu Dalconzo for your guidance throughout my journey.

Contents

Prologue

My intention for this book is for you to have a comprehensive understanding about your ego mind, which is an organ of the soul. The ego mind makes a great servant, but a lousy master. When we understand how it works exactly, it becomes easier to master it.

The ego often gets a bad rap, but the truth is that the ego mind is one of the most valuable assets for a human being. Thank you to our ego mind!

Most of the concepts being presented came from my extensive training at Holistic Learning Center and from their textbook, "Self Mastery, A Journey Home to your Inner Self" by Hu Dalconzo. Having studied, practiced and facilitated the lessons in this book for over ten years, I wanted to offer some of my perspectives of the ego mind.

I hope you will find the content relatable, and discover that you're not alone as you embark upon the quest of mastering your ego mind. Keep in mind that the ego mind is not a monster or a presence within you that is insurmountable. It is actually pretty humorous and means no real harm. When you align with the ego and value its work by understanding and taking charge of its defense mechanisms, it is more likely to serve you.

Introduction

Welcome to 101 Insights about the Ego Mind. My name is Sharda Geer, and I am thrilled to bring you the insights about the ego that I have come to understand over the years.

To share a little about myself: I started on the path of meditation and self discovery during childhood in the 80's, and embarked on the journey of self transformation around 2005. It was a road of many breakdowns and breakthroughs as I uncovered the various layers of what makes up the human being. My adult journey started with the discovery of organic food and natural healing, which led me to visiting my very first Holistic Physician and Holistic Gynecologist. I then learned about Quantum Biofeedback and other Quantum healing tools.

As my past started to reveal itself to me through my understanding of how blocked emotions led to the illnesses in my body and mind, I was determined to unlock the healing powers within me.

I attended several transformational intensive workshops that helped me experience my authentic self in a way I never did before. I found myself in a state of driven bliss. Naturally, I wanted to learn the art of eliciting this kind of feeling in others. And so, I ventured into Coaching.

After an exhaustive search, I was blessed to discover Holistic Learning Center, an online Coaching Certification School with a 1-year training and 2-year internship. I graduated from the full program as a Certified Spiritual Life Coach in January 2014. I continued to study and practice Energy healing work and other forms of coaching.

Through my journey, I realized and resolved many of the underlying causes of depression, anxiety, uterine issues, migraines, auto-immune disease and more. Because of that, I now consider them to be blessings.

I learned about the laws that govern our lives here on earth, and like any game, until we study and understand its rules, we will continue to experience loss and have a miserable time- no fun. Mastering the laws of life and learning how to live within them is a life-long process that often feels like a roller-coaster. Thankfully, like any good roller-coaster ride, there are pauses too, even if right after a pause, the ride then goes backwards in the dark LOL.

Before you dive in, though, I would like to let you in on a little secret: the points in this book aren't numbered. If this idea makes you feel uneasy, frustrated or even a bit triggered, congratulations- you're already having your first encounter with the ego mind! Not to worry though, its just your ego mind having a little tantrum. Take a few breaths, embrace the chaos and enjoy the insights.

1

The ego mind is your protector

- When you were a small child and you started to experience discomfort in your life, your ego mind immediately stepped in, ready to protect your tender psyche.

- To protect you, it made you wrong in order to make your care-givers right because it knew that you needed them for food, clothing and shelter–otherwise you would've died as an infant. Think about how you would feel now about someone who saved you from starvation. For the most part, we make it so that they can do no wrong. This is the same principle which the ego mind acted upon towards your parents when you were a child. It is a principle based on the natural human psychological process known as Parental Idealization.

- The ego will suppress any experience it believes to be painful. If or when you attempt to access those memories, it will most likely not let you recall them, or will distort, minimize and dismiss them as nothing. For example, today, you might experience road rage from the moment you encounter another vehicle to the moment you arrive at your destination. But if you decide to address the root cause of this pattern by looking at your childhood experiences, you might declare that you had a great childhood with no connection to the current road rage, which is likely untrue. Your ego will likely retort with the response: "It's the other drivers! If they would learn how to drive, I wouldn't have road rage!"

- Unconscious emotional over-connectedness with your parents and caregivers beyond childhood years is your ego's way of secretly keeping you from taking full responsibility for your life. This is shown by being unclear on what your own likes and dislikes are, or what your beliefs are compared to your parents'. As long as you are emotionally over-connected, you will find it difficult or nearly impossible to discover your true nature and identity.

2

The ego mind- friend or foe?

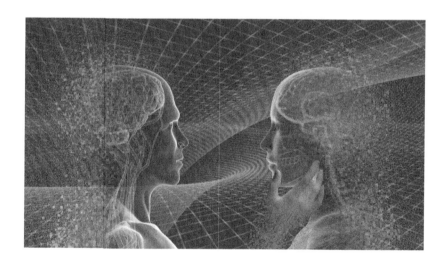

· If you believe all of the lies the ego mind constructed during your childhood, it will always make you right. For example, let's say that you received a bad grade in Math when you were a child, and your parents punished you and declared that you would amount to nothing. In this situation, due to parental idealization, your ego would have been forced to make them right and you wrong. It would've done that by suppressing the feeling of anger or hurt you felt in that moment, and form the belief that "I'm not smart, that's why they punished me." Over time, this will most likely morph into more solid beliefs such as "I'm not good enough," or "I have to be perfect in order to be loved". Later, as a fully functioning adult, these beliefs will likely play out in the form of you over-working due to your ego convincing you that you have no choice. However, as an adult, unless these beliefs are addressed and determined as false, the ego mind will continue to convince you otherwise, and keep you stuck in the cycles created by the false beliefs.

· The ego is like a chameleon. It takes what exists in its environment and creates a protective framework of beliefs that ensures your survival. Let's say that as a child you were yelled at or punished for drawing on the walls. You would have experienced the yelling or punishment as traumatizing, which would have consequently created a wound. Your ego mind would then decide what would be an acceptable defense in that type of environment. It might decide to feed you thoughts, such as "I can't be creative," or "If I scream loudly, they will leave me alone," or "If I cry, they will feel sorry for me and be kind.'' In the future, this might look like a lack of confidence in your ability to do art, or believing that nobody would find it valuable. This would inhibit you from pursuing art, even if you feel it's your passion.

- The ego mind is like the internet. When you search a situation, it will pull up all the evidence it has collected over the years about it. The ego then justifies why its beliefs are still true and relevant now even if they no longer are. For example, if you would like to get married, it will promptly provide all the stories of past marriages from your family and community members, or the divorce statistics you read a few years ago of the entire country! If your parents had an unhappy marriage and you have already decided you never want to experience that, the ego might form the conclusion that all marriages lead to unhappiness.

3

The ego mind as the Identity Generator

- The ego mind has two major functions that start in your childhood years:

(a) to create protective mechanisms (discussed above and more to follow)
(b) to create identities or personalities in order for you to function in the world

- The function of creating identities is one that requires higher intelligence. The elements of an identity are thoughts, feelings, actions, beliefs and belief systems. It is our identities that eventually create our realities.

- Beliefs are formed based on the actual and perceived experience in a given moment. Beliefs are also formed based on the path you came here to walk, which includes your purpose and your mission. Therefore, the identities or personalities the ego mind creates are also in accordance with your purpose and mission here on earth. These beliefs and identities also include the defense mechanisms because they are part of the purpose of your incarnation. For example, if you experienced abandonment as a child, one of your ego defenses might be suspicion of others when they make promises or not trusting others easily. This could also lead to self-reliance at an early age. Later, as an adult, you might find you are passionate about helping adopted children build resilience. You might discover that this is your purpose and mission.

- The ego mind creates many personalities. Just as we require different outfits for different activities we engage in, we require different personalities for different roles we play in life. We might utilize a certain identity for the workplace, and a certain one for hanging out with friends on the weekend.

· During our childhood developmental years, the ego mind would have created a Core Fear-based Identity in an attempt to help the child navigate its circumstances.

· The ego mind has the ability to adapt and evolve its identities in changing circumstances and situations. This adaptability helps you to integrate new experiences, growth, and development. However, the elements of the Core-Fear Identity will infiltrate any new identities created thereafter.

4

Your ego mind as your master

- The ego mind is incredibly loud and doesn't stop talking! It just goes on and on until you believe it. Once you believe it, it starts to tell you how wrong you are for believing it.

- It has a contradictory nature and cannot always be trusted with the relevant truth. For example, if you want to start a business, it might say, "You won't make it". But if your spouse challenges you with a similar line, it might then say, "I'll show you!" This dynamic would be based on things that are no longer relevant in your life, such as past sibling rivalry or peer pressure. It would keep you from seeing the possible importance of your spouse's concerns.

- The ego mind must be right! Even if it contradicts itself! It might say something like, "If it's going to get done right, I'll have to do it myself!" But when you become exhausted and can't get it done, it might say "See, you're not good enough."

- When you continue to believe your ego mind's stories to be the relevant truth for you now, the ego mind has become your master. The way to break free from its shackles is to realize that the stories were a necessary truth that you needed to believe as a child, not as an adult.

- The ego mind will convince you that your sense of self, self-worth and inner happiness are attached to external sources, thereby disconnecting you from your inner resources and keeping you as its slave.

5

The ego mind vs Self (Intuitive self)

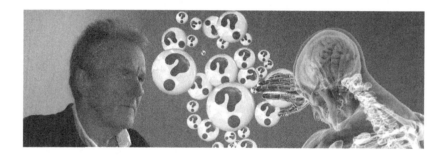

· The ego mind is often loud and fast, and floods your mind with an influx of thoughts. The Self, comparatively, has a soft tone and often communicates a single message.

· There are times when you must listen to what the ego mind is saying because it is telling you about the childhood wounds it is protecting. Then you will know which of your powers you can use to heal.

- The ego can be re-programmed through visualizations and new affirmative language. The ego mind cannot tell if what you are visualizing is actually happening or not. This allows you to re-visualize traumatizing experiences even from your distant past and heal them.

- If you think of chewing on a lemon, immediately your mouth will begin to salivate even though you're not actually eating a lemon. Likewise, when your Self embarks on a healing process, it can utilize its power of visualization to emerge the multi-sensory memory of the trauma, and use the adult powers it has now to re-parent the child. It can give the child permission to say 'NO!" or to feel and release its feelings, thereby leaving the child feeling empowered. The Self is always in charge and can change the effect of the past on the psyche to one that is empowering and liberating.

6

The ego mind vs feelings

· One of the ego mind's child-like defense mechanisms is to keep you
  from feeling your actual feelings. Remember when I referred to the

ego as a chameleon? This is one example of how it functions as one. Many of us grew up in environments where we were not allowed to show our feelings, especially anger, sadness or hurt. Anger was often seen as violent, sadness as depression, and hurt as weakness. As such, the ego mind would decide to use the defense mechanism of repressing the feeling via fear-based thoughts about the feeling. Below are some of the ways the ego mind does this.

· The ego wouldn't block the feelings we learned how to express without pain. But for the feelings you would have experienced disapproval or some discomfort from as a child, the ego would block you from feeling them, now as well.

· When something ends, such as when a relationship ends, you will naturally feel sad. When you feel and release the sad feelings, you are better able to understand the ending as a possible gift in your life. But instead, the ego mind will block you with fear-based thoughts of self-pity. This will often lead to an emotional state of depression, which can be easier for others to understand and accept.

· When your boundaries are violated, you will naturally feel angry. Ideally, your next step would be to feel, process, and express your anger maturely, and appropriately protect your boundaries. But the ego mind will promptly block you from feeling anger with its fear-based thoughts of blame and betrayal, causing you to act inappropriately.

- When you are about to start something new in your life, you will tend to feel scared or nervous. When you feel and process those scared feelings, you will be able to embrace the new venture. But the ego will often block the scared feeling with over-thinking, which causes you to experience confusion and keeps you from confidently taking action to move forward. Then you will likely start to experience hopelessness.

- Frustration is a feeling that surfaces when something is taking longer than you expected. When you actually feel frustration, you would naturally want to release it or express it in the form of persistence so that you would see the project through to the end. However, you might often run into the wall of judgment against yourself or others about why something is taking so long, which eventually leads to a sense of feeling dissatisfied with yourself, your life and others.

- When you feel disappointed, what is often needed is for you to appropriately detach from the person or situation. Instead, the ego mind will surface fear-based thoughts from the past, causing you to be indecisive and leaving you feeling discouraged.

- Worry is a feeling you experience when you need to make appropriate preparations for a situation. The ego would often block this feeling with thoughts telling you to avoid what needs to be done, thus resulting in procrastination. Over time, you are left feeling a sense of helplessness.

- Anxiety occurs when the ego mind is surfacing fear-based thoughts from the past or ones about the future about the fear you're actually feeling. However, the fear is simply trying to warn you of something, or indicating that you're about to learn something new. When you stay in the energy of anxiety, you end up feeling crippled and overwhelmed by the uncertainty you're facing.

- Perfectionism is the ego-manifested block against feelings of embarrassment which surfaces when you need to be in a place of self-acceptance of your less-than-preferred actions. When you allow perfectionism to consume you, you eventually begin to believe you are inadequate.

- Feeling hurt is scary to the ego, and so it blocks those feelings with thoughts of self pity, leaving you feeling alone and isolated. What you actually need is to fully understand yourself.

· The psyche toggles between envy and jealousy. Envy is a feeling that serves to motivate you to achieve something you want that you've seen in another person. Jealousy is the ego mind's way of blocking envy. When you believe the ego mind, you end up feeling resentful towards the other person, and an overall sense of being deprived of what you want and deserve.

· When you feel a sense of indifference, you might find that it started at the time when something ended, a time of sorrow. When sorrow is felt and released, it becomes an energy that helps you grieve the loss and extract its blessings. Without doing this, you might start to feel powerless, indifferent, cold, and withdrawn from the sweetness of life.

· Shame is a feeling that is surfaced when you do something to feel remorseful for. But often, you might find that thoughts of guilt take over. This solves nothing. What would serve you is to feel and release the shame so that you are motivated to change. Guilt doesn't foster positive change, it only invites more fear and creates more of the same unwanted behavior.

· The ego mind is your defender, it is your best friend or like your attorney. It will always do what it thinks will help you.

- You now get to teach your ego mind new tools and methods of protecting you. Tools like forgiveness, healthy boundaries and more.

7

The ego mind gone unconscious

· Part of the function of the ego mind is to allow certain memories to go unconscious. Those experiences that were too traumatic for the young psyche were kept in a part of the mind that you cannot consciously or readily access. It does this because it wants to protect you. It means no harm.

· Because of this ability to keep memories at the unconscious level, unprocessed feelings are also buried along with the memories. This could leave you feeling numb and stuck in a mental fog about why you keep doing the same things over and over.

8

The ego mind in relationships

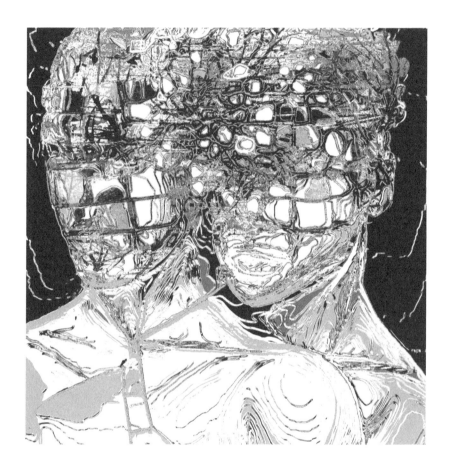

· We get into relationships, and as we get closer, we realize a different person is emerging. Who is it? Who are they? And who am I?

· Our dear friend, the ego, starts to feel safe and comfortable to show its characteristics to its friend, which is the other person's ego. They recognize each other's traits and decide to have a go at it! YES, the battle of the egos!

- Our egos would get into an argument of blaming either ego for its ways!

- We are mirrors of each other's egos. When our ego is triggered by the other person's egoic behavior, it is most likely because our ego possesses the same trait, even if it's in a different form.

- When we feel triggered by our partners' actions, it is the wound that the ego is protecting that is being triggered. And if the trigger lasts more than an hour, that means that the wound is unhealed. Yes, the trigger lets us know what we get to address within ourselves.

- We must realize that we are not always just in a relationship with the true essence of the other person. Nor are they in a relationship with just our true essence.

- When the ego goes into blame, judgment, criticism, harshness, or needing to be right, it is like we're in a tango with each other's egos. There cannot be a tango with just one dancer.

- The ego mind loves to conspire with another about a different person's egoic behavior in an attempt to be righteous, as though it always displays perfect behavior itself.

9

The ego mind in career

· The ego resists growth and change!

- You might hear the ego's resistance in this way: "Have you lost your mind?!" "Growth?!" "NO!"

- It sees change and growth as threats to the constructs it created to keep you safe when you were a helpless child.

- "The ego is never happy. In the winter, it longs for summer; in the summer, it longs for winter" - Self mastery, A journey home to your inner self by Hu Dalconzo.

- The ego becomes uneasy when it doesn't have anything, and when it has everything.

- The ego makes the important unimportant and the unimportant important.

- The more opportunities presented, the more the ego mind will come up with anything it can to try to sabotage them.

10

The ego mind's defense mechanisms

· The ego mind disappears when the body is under threat. It takes the back seat and gets quiet. For example, in the moment when we are startled and become frightened, our physiological survival mechanism kicks in, and the ego's survival construct goes quiet.

· The ego mind is like the "skin" of your soul. It serves to protect the soul and its organs, just as the skin protects the inner organs of the body.

· The ego mind is addicted to excitement. It will create an environment of drama, such as looking for ways to be right about how others or the world is wrong, and then it will make a huge deal out of it. It will tell everyone it can about what happened, creating a mountain out of a molehill.

· Its addiction to excitement also shows up in the form of self aware- ness or self realization. It is exciting for the ego as you become passionate about understanding the ego and yourself. If you let the ego's excitement take charge, you will soon discover that self realization does not equal self transformation. The ego will use this excitement to keep you addicted to learning instead of implementing, robbing you of the joy and exuberance you are searching for.

· The ego thrives in its construct of F.E.A.R. (False Evidence Appearing Real). For example, it will convince you that it is not safe to rely on your own intuition. The reasons for that are kept from your conscious mind, but they play out in your subconscious mind with the memory of when your mom's intuition was wrong 35 years ago when you were 2 years old and she blamed your dad, resulting in a fight between them. Your ego mind will convince you that your intuition is therefore always wrong and that you cannot trust it.

· The ego mind is dualistic and processes life in a polarized way - there is no gray area. It uses limitations in extremities such as "right and wrong" or "good and bad."

· The ego mind is an energy that separates. It separates you from the awareness of yourself. It separates you from your feelings, and it separates you from your higher intelligence.

· The ego mind uses rationalization, denial, minimizing, and dismissal about what you're experiencing now in order to keep you from uncovering the truth about the past, and the defenses it came up with back then that are not working for you now.

· When you embark on the journey of mastering your ego, it will creatively manifest itself in convincing and subtle ways such as illnesses or super busy-ness in order to keep you from continuing the journey.

- The ego mind does not like to be held accountable, or be seen to have made a mistake. It must always be right.

11

The ego mind as your comfort zone

· Ah yes! Let's hang out on the couch! The ego mind loves comfort zones. After all, it has worked hard to keep you sane and safe from infancy through adolescence, and now it wants life to stay that way. How dare you seek out growth and change?!

· But even in the comfort zone, it will not stop talking. It will always have something to say. Something negative, fear-based, confusing and contradicting.

· The ego mind creates frameworks which hold stories and opinions about you, life, and everyone it has met or heard about throughout your life. Therefore, if a person should grow, or a situation improve, the ego mind will become very uncomfortable and attempt to make them wrong for changing.

12

Ego Defenses in adult life (Virtue vs Vice)

· The ego mind uses your divine qualities as its fear-based defenses to protect you. For example, it can use your natural quality of sweetness to make you act timid, ensuring that you are liked by everyone. This comes as a cost to your growth, where you could be developing your yang powers to be bold as needed.

· Below are possible ways this function of the ego mind could show up in your life.

· Divine quality: Acceptance

Ego's defense: Settling for less
  Payoff: Appearing humble
  Cost to growth: Taking life to next level

· Divine quality: Agreeable

Ego's defense: Fear of objecting
  Payoff: Peace
  Cost to growth: Healthy discussions and the permission to disagree

· Divine quality: Care

Ego's defense: Controlling
  Payoff: I get to be right

Cost to growth: Learning to live on your own terms and accept the same of others

· Divine quality: Commitment to Self-awareness

Ego's defense: Self-help addiction
   Payoff: I am better than the average person
   Cost to growth: Inclusiveness and implementing the knowledge

· Divine quality: Compassion

Ego's defense: Taking on others' troubles as your own
   Payoff: Appearing Always has friends, and is needed and liked
   Cost to growth: Allowing space for the other person to discover their own strengths and solutions

· Divine quality: Confidence

Ego's defense: Arrogance, a know-it-all
   Payoff: Admiration from others and a resource for information
   Cost to growth: Being open to learning and growing, exchange of love and wisdom

· Divine quality: Constructive feedback

Ego's defense: Criticizing
   Payoff: A good leader

Cost to growth: Ability to truly understand and appreciate others

- Divine quality: Contentment

Ego's defense: Stagnation
    Payoff: Don't have to face failure
    Cost to growth: Risk-taking skulls, growth in of itself

- Divine quality: Cooperative

Ego's defense: Overly helpful
    Payoff: Feeling needed
    Cost to growth: Learning how to identify what a person actually needs and maybe teach them how to give it to themselves (teach a person how to fish vs giving them the fish)

- Divine quality: Dedication to growth

Ego's defense: Ego-righteousness
    Payoff: Looking good to others
    Cost to growth: Actual growth

- Divine quality: Endurance

Ego's defense: Over-working
    Payoff: Praise/rewards
    Cost to growth: Making a difference where it really matters

· Divine quality: Energetic

Ego's defense: Overly busy
  Payoff: People leave you alone
  Cost to growth: Facing the truth you're avoiding

· Divine quality: Forgiveness

Ego's defense: Excusing bad behavior
  Payoff: Looks good and continues to live in what is familiar
  Cost to growth: Honesty and accountability in relationships

· Divine quality: Generosity

Ego's defense: Doing or giving more than is needed or affordable
  Payoff: Looking good and receiving praise
  Cost to growth: Leadership skills. Learning to say no. Honoring another person's abilities.

· Divine quality: Happiness

Ego's defense: Excess joking or laughing
  Payoff: People will like me
  Cost to growth: Healing inner wounds that are blocking actual happiness

· Divine quality: Honesty

Ego's defense:Attacking/Judging or using the truth as a sword
   Payoff: No one messes with me
   Cost to growth: Discernment and responsible communication skills

- Divine quality: Humility

Ego's defense: Not accepting praise, insecurity
   Payoff: Will always fit in by playing small
   Cost to growth: Not living to one's true potential

- Divine quality: Kindness

Ego's defense: People-pleasing
   Payoff: Never having to face rejection by saying "no"
   Cost to growth: Healthy boundaries

- Divine quality:Leadership

Ego's defense: Dictating or bossiness
   Payoff: Others obey
   Cost to growth: Learning to be a servant leader

- Divine quality:Love

Ego's defense: Worry
   Payoff: I'm a good person/parent

Cost to growth: Learning to take charge of one's own life and to teach others to do the same

· Divine quality:Loyalty

Ego's defense: Over-doing, over-working
  Payoff: Praise/promotion
  Cost to growth: Healthy boundaries, self love

· Divine quality: Peace

Ego's defense: Avoidance
  Payoff: Appearance of being accommodating and understanding
  Cost to growth: Authentic communication

· Divine quality: Patience

Ego's defense: Fear of being honest, low standards
  Payoff: We all appear to get along, being understanding
  Cost to growth: Courage to be honest, having high standards

· Divine quality: Positive attitude

Ego's defense: Being oblivious
  Payoff: Liked by others, appears innocent
  Cost to growth: Ability to see the whole picture and act appropriately with discernment

· Divine quality: Purity

Ego's defense: Celibacy
   Payoff: Assumed holiness and regard from others
   Cost to growth: Experiencing the ecstasy of living in equilibrium, a purified state of consciousness

· Divine quality: Resilience

Ego's defense: Fear of appearing weak
   Payoff: Praise and reward for being strong
   Cost to growth: Living life on one's own terms

· Divine quality: Respect

Ego's defense: Fearful
   Payoff: Approval and acceptance from others
   Cost to growth: Self dignity and self respect

· Divine quality:Responsibility

Ego's defense: Blame
   Payoff: Pity, importance
   Cost to growth: Accountability, balance, leadership skills

· Divine quality: Self-discipline

Ego's defense: Rigidity
  Payoff: Success
  Cost to growth: Flexibility and balance

  · Divine quality: Tolerance

Ego's defense: Enabling
  Payoff: Praise for being tolerant
  Cost to growth: Space for you and the other person to grow

  · Divine quality: Trust

Ego's defense: Gullible
  Payoff: Loved
  Cost to growth: Trust building skills to earn and give trust appropriately

The ego mind will show its true colors to the ones closest to it.

13

Discover your Self

Who am I anyway?

Am I the roles and responsibilities I fulfill, such as parent, student, daughter, son, CEO? If that is who I am, then who am I when the CEO takes a vacation with the family? Do I cease to exist? Or is that I simply stepped into a different role?

Am I the feelings that I experience? When I say I am joyful, then when something happens and I feel hurt, do I cease to exist? Or is it that I'm experiencing a different emotion?

Am I the thoughts I am having? The mind says I am a good person. Then I react poorly to my loved one that contradicts the mind's definition of a "good person". Do I then cease to exist? Or did I simply have a human response to a stimulus?

Am I the body? I might say I am a male or a female or identify with a gender. But when the body dies, do I cease to exist? If I did, why do I say "Rest In Peace?". Who will be resting in peace? Who is the loved one I am hoping will still be pleased with me or bless me or look out for me from above?

Am I the physical experiences I am having? For example, I think I am hearing impaired, or I am autistic, I'm handicapped. What does that say about the folks that hear well and don't have a physical handicap? Do they not exist? Or when my own hearing is improved or resolved, do I cease to exist?

Could it be that I am the eternal life force that is constant within this human body, and doesn't change but simply has an experience of the mental body, feeling body, senses and physical body? Could it be that these are simply the organs of "I?"

What if the essence of I, because it is not any of the manifestations, has power over its organs? What would that actually mean in practical life?

It would mean that I can observe the experiences and can direct each organ (mind, feelings, senses and body) what to do or how to be. It

51

means that I can help them to process and understand what they're experiencing, and make it a better environment to dwell in.

It could mean that I would be free to channel the wisdom of the infinite intelligence and bring that wisdom to my organs and enhance my human experience.

14

How to train your ego mind to be your servant

W hen training your ego mind, you could start with simple exercises you know would serve you well. Be aware, though, that the ego would resist routines of self-discipline and self-care. The ego does not like change but is also very easily bored. For example, if you decide that you would practice 15 minutes of mindfulness every morning at 6:00 AM, your ego will enjoy that for a few days and then it will give you reasons why you shouldn't do it or can't do it. Do it anyway.

Breathing - Taking deep inhalations, holding your breath and then slow exhalations for 3-6 minutes while focusing on the breath. The ego does not like breathing exercises, particularly when you decide to focus on the breath and for a certain count or time frame. Oh dear! The ego goes nuts! It'll distract your focus to something else and say it's not helping, keeping you from your daily practice. Do it anyway :-).

Breath is life, it is the evidence that you are alive. It is the connection between the life force that is you and the Universal Intelligence that makes all of life possible.

Meditation - There are many forms of meditation. The form that best trains your ego mind is where you sit in one place with a specific focus for a certain period of time, even just for 5 minutes. You could choose to focus on an object or thought.

Feelings first, thoughts second - As mentioned previously, if you listen to your ego mind first, it will surface thoughts to block your feelings. Recognize your feelings as an uncomfortable physical sensation first. Release it through conscious breathing, then engage the mind's solutions.

Keep your word - The ego-mind would much rather you listen to and obey its instructions. When you, the intelligence within, commits to something and you keep that commitment no matter what, the ego mind starts to learn who is in charge.

Accountability - The ego mind would compel you to find an alternative explanation to a mistake and possibly make it someone else's fault. As an adult, you get to own your mistakes from a healed and mature place, knowing that you have the power to see your flaws and correct them with kindness and compassion for the purpose of growth and evolution.

Reading - Reading expands self-awareness. It also helps to relax the ego because it knows you're learning. It is learning too. So, be cognizant of that. The ego can cause you to become addicted to only learning, thereby preventing you from implementing what you're learning to a level of mastery and affirming that you are not good enough or broken. Read, learn, evolve.

Grow - Oh, how the ego mind would repulse this! Growth is the opposite of what the ego mind is. Growth brings uncertainty to the ego mind. It also means that you will discover all its tricks and games and change them. Commit to growth to heal from the past, and develop your natural abilities to create the life you want.

Journaling - Journaling will help you to see things you wouldn't have otherwise.

Use your powers as divine resources and not the version the ego-mind generated as defense mechanisms when you were a powerless child. You are naturally infused with goodness. You are equipped with both feminine (yin) and masculine (yang) charged energies. They are all divine in nature.

Learn the tools and techniques to use them as such. They are best experienced when in balance. With the appropriate yang energy, which is a protective energy, the yin energies are free to emerge. Too much or too little of either will be an unpleasant experience. For example, if there is too much assertiveness (yang) without thoughtfulness (yin), then that behavior can be experienced as aggressive. If there is too much thoughtfulness without a commitment to a specific goal or outcome, then that behavior can be experienced as scattered or unable to complete tasks.

Adult permissions – As an adult, you now have the power to give yourself the permission to live life for your highest and greatest good. Simple permissions to like what you like, or to play and have fun, or to say no or yes will enrich your life and start to quiet the ego mind. It will realize that you are taking your rightful place in determining what is suitable for your life.

15

Conclusion

The ego mind is an invaluable part of the human psyche because it's job is to protect and defend. It is highly intelligent and dedicated to making our lives successful on earth. However, without having clear directions, it will always default to fear. It will also take over and run things until we awaken to our responsibility and take charge. When we do, we must honor our ego mind as we teach it to fulfill its duties as our servant. The ego will lower its defenses against us when we consistently show up powerfully. It will learn to trust our ability to run the show as long as we lovingly and maturely heal our inner pain and allow the little powerless parts of ourselves to heal and grow. The ego mind will continue to remind us of our duties and responsibility to our inner children whether we understand it or not, or whether we want to address it or not.

The identities our ego-mind creates are based on how we processed the feelings that surfaced at a specific moment in our lives. . The manner in which we processed our feelings would have determined the actions and behavior we created, which in turn determined the beliefs that were generated. These are the elements that go into forming our identities. And it is through our identities that we design the realities we live in.

The function of the ego mind is also based on the reason we took this incarnation. It creates identities and defense mechanisms in accordance with our karmic (life lessons) and dharmic (life purpose) curricula. Like I said, it is highly intelligent. But it is designed to be a servant, not a master. We, the divine intelligence, are the master. Let us step up and take charge!

If you've found this book helpful, I'd be very appreciative if you left a favorable review for the book on Amazon.

Resources

Holistic Learning Centers. (2024, May 24). *Self-Mastery, a journey home to your inner self - holistic learning centers.* https://www.holisticle arningcenter.com/product/self-mastery-a-journey-home-to-your-inner-self

Holistic Learning Centers. (2022, July 19). *The HUMAN Handbook - Holistic Learning Centers.* https://www.holisticlearningcenter.com/pro duct/human-handbook

Made in the USA
Las Vegas, NV
10 July 2024

92129035R00039